The Tragedy of the
Titanic

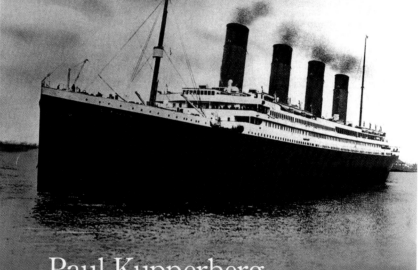

Paul Kupperberg

the rosen publishing group's
rosen central

To Robin

Published in 2003 by The Rosen Publishing Group, Inc.
29 East 21st Street, New York, NY 10010

First Edition

Library of Congress Cataloging-in-Publication Data

Kupperberg, Paul.
The tragedy of the *Titanic* / Paul Kupperberg. — 1st ed.
    p. cm. — (When disaster strikes!)
Summary: Recounts the sinking of the *Titanic* in 1912, events leading up to the tragedy, the inquiry that followed, and ongoing interest in the story and wreckage of the luxurious passenger ship called unsinkable.
Includes bibliographical references (p.   ).
ISBN 0-8239-3679-1 (lib. bdg.)
1. *Titanic* (Steamship)—Juvenile literature. 2. Shipwrecks—North Atlantic Ocean—Juvenile literature. [1. *Titanic* (Steamship) 2. Shipwrecks.]
I. Title. II. When disaster strikes! (New York, N.Y.)
G530.T6 K87 2002
910'.9163'4—dc21

                                                                2001008527

Manufactured in the United States of America

On the cover:
The bow of the *Titanic* lies on the ocean floor some 12,500 feet beneath the surface of the North Atlantic.
Title page and cover inset:
This photo of the *Titanic* was taken in April 1912 as the ship was leaving port for her first—and final—voyage.

Contents

The evacuation of the *Titanic* was very poorly managed, inefficient, and at times chaotic. There were not nearly enough lifeboats for the ship's passengers, and most of the lifeboats were not full when they were lowered into the sea.

Introduction

April, 1912.
It was a time in which industrialized nations such as the United States and England felt they could achieve anything they set their minds to. The modern technological age was still in its infancy, but in little more than a single generation, science and technology had advanced further and faster than they had in the thousand years before. The Industrial Revolution had ushered in power-driven machines that began to replace manual labor and greatly expand the amount of goods that could be produced and the speed with which they could be made. Horse-drawn carts and carriages had yielded to automobiles. Candle and firelight had been replaced by electricity. Manufacturing and commerce surpassed agriculture as the dominant economic forces in the United States.

The turn of the twentieth century was marked by a flurry of technological advances—each more awe-inspiring than the last—with the potential to change the lives of every man, woman, and child in the world. Improvements in steel manufacturing and the invention of the elevator paved the way for the construction of towering skyscrapers in cities such as Chicago and New York. The transcontinental railroad and the automobile had opened the entire country up to more comfortable, faster travel over much greater distances. The electric-powered New York City subway (and similar regional transportation systems around the country) made local travel possible for anyone possessing the relatively modest five-cent fare. Perhaps the most revolutionary and breathtaking modern marvel of all up to that point, the airplane, had been born at the dawn of the new century and would profoundly alter the way people traveled, worked, and waged war.

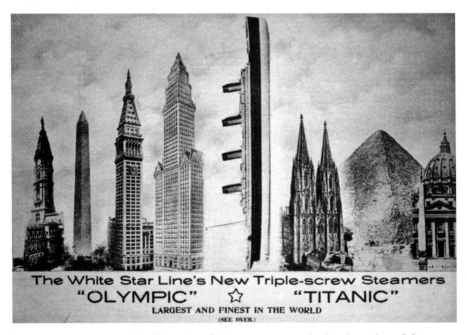

The White Star Line's New Triple-screw Steamers
"OLYMPIC" ☆ "TITANIC"
LARGEST AND FINEST IN THE WORLD
(SEE OVER.)

This drawing compares the length of the *Titanic* with the height of famous buildings, including the Egyptian pyramids and the Washington Monument.

WARNINGS IGNORED

The radio operator of the steamer *Mesaba* to the *Titanic*'s radio operator

Mesaba: "Ice report . . . Saw much heavy pack ice and great number large icebergs, also field ice. Weather good, clear."

Titanic: "Received, thanks."

The radio operator of the *Californian* to the *Titanic*'s radio operator

Californian: "Say, old man, we are stopped and surrounded by ice."

Titanic: "Shut up! Shut up! I am busy."

Recorded in *Titanic: An Illustrated History*

Consumer goods of all kinds were being made faster, better, and cheaper on high-speed production lines. The rich were richer than ever, and more people were struggling out of poverty to join the growing middle class. For this reason, it was an era known as the Gilded Age. It was a breathtaking, exhilarating time for most people. The feeling was one of unlimited optimism, a future promising an unending parade of scientific and technological wonders, innovations that might just lead all citizens into a utopia of prosperity, good health, and material comfort. The belief was that anything that could be conceived could be built, and all of humanity would benefit as a result.

Into this brave and confident new world of technology sailed the *Titanic*, an enormous symbol of modernity's astounding achievements—and its fatal shortcomings.

The Unsinkable Titanic

The *Titanic* was an accurate reflection of the times in which she was created. She was at once a product of the stiff, class-conscious formality of the nineteenth century on the one hand and the more free-wheeling energy of the electric new century on the other. The *Titanic* was both the largest and the most luxurious passenger ship ever built.

Sailing in Style

In an age when the social standing of the wealthy was judged by the extravagance of their travel arrangements, standards could not have been higher on the *Titanic*, at least not for the 329 first-class passengers. This privileged group sailed in luxurious suites and cabins high above the waterline and were permitted unlimited access to gourmet dining rooms, salons, and luxury decks. They were waited on hand and foot by valets, stewards, maids, barbers, waiters, kitchen staff, and a masseuse, not to mention any personal servants they brought along with them. First-class staterooms were available in any one of seven architectural styles. Each first-class suite contained a sitting room, two bedrooms, two wardrobe rooms, and a private bathroom.

The *Titanic*'s 285 second-class passengers may not have had it quite as good as their first-class counterparts, but their accommodations aboard the *Titanic* were anything but squalid. Even the 710 third-class (or steerage) passengers kept below decks, out of sight of the expensive first-class accommodations (which cost as much as $4,350 in 1912, or approximately $80,000 today), were more comfortable in their relatively tight quarters aboard the *Titanic* than passengers on similar ships of the day ever were. Sailing in steerage generally meant crossing the Atlantic in a dank, dirty, densely packed, disease-ridden below-decks hold of a heaving, creaking ship.

Wednesday, April 10

12:00 PM

The *Titanic* departs Southampton, England, and stops at ports in France and Ireland before setting sail for New York.

Building the *Titanic*

The *Titanic*, along with her sister ship, the *Olympic*, was commissioned by Britain's White Star steamship line and constructed by the shipbuilders Harland and Wolff of Belfast, Ireland. The builders were given an unlimited budget and orders to create the largest, most magnificent ship ever. At an eventual cost of some $7.5 million (approximately $137 million in today's dollars), they delivered the floating palace that White Star had requested.

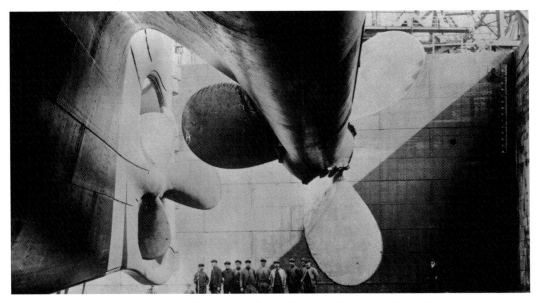

The *Titanic*'s massive propellers dwarf workers before her launch. The center propeller had four sixteen-foot blades, and the left and right propellers each had three blades that were twenty-three and one-half feet in diameter.

Like the *Olympic*, the *Titanic* was 882.5 feet long (a football field is 300 feet, a modern aircraft carrier around 900 feet) and 92.5 feet wide at its beam, but the *Titanic* beat out the *Olympic* for the honors as the largest liner in the world by 1,004 tons, weighing in at a colossal 46,328 tons. She carried twenty-nine boilers, each fifteen feet tall and weighing 100 tons, which could produce a maximum of 55,000 horsepower to drive her two sets of four-cylinder reciprocating engines at speeds up to twenty-three knots. This made the *Titanic* the biggest, fastest luxury liner to ever sail the seas.

The magnificent ship stood 175 feet tall from her keel to the top of her distinctive four funnels. Only three of the funnels, or smokestacks, were real; the fourth was a dummy placed on the ship to balance out the design and was used for ventilation. There were ten decks to carry as many as 3,547 passengers and 908 officers and crew. She carried sixteen lifeboats and four collapsible boats, far fewer than necessary to accommodate such a large passenger list. The *Titanic* was considered unsinkable, so it was thought that unnecessary lifeboats would only clutter the decks.

The Lap of Luxury

The *Titanic* was outfitted in the most luxurious style imaginable. The ship's centerpiece was a grand staircase (one of two first-class staircases) crafted of polished oak and decorated with a bronze cherub, an ornate clock, oil paintings, and gold-plated light fixtures. Her railings were made of wrought iron and gilt bronze. During the day, the grand staircase's landing was flooded with natural light pouring in from a domed overhead skylight. The first-class public spaces were richly

Sunday, April 14

8:40 PM

Second Officer Lightoller orders a sharp lookout for icebergs after the *Titanic* receives four ice warnings in twelve hours.

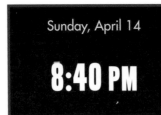

furnished and decorated. This included a first-class lounge with mahogany and mother of pearl paneling (modeled after the French royal palace at Versailles), a smoking room fitted with stained-glass windows, a 100-foot-long dining salon, the Verandah Café (complete with ivy growing up its walls and decorated with wicker furniture), and the Café Parisien (modeled after a French sidewalk café). In addition, a reading and writing room, a swimming pool (which the *Titanic* and the *Olympic* were the first steamships to feature), a Turkish bath, a barber shop, a squash court, a gymnasium, and four electric elevators were provided for the comfort of passengers.

This elegant staircase led to the *Titanic*'s first-class salon.

"We heard the order, 'All men stand back away from the boats' . . . The men all stood away and waited in absolute silence, some leaning against the railings of the deck, others pacing slowly up and down . . . The women got in quietly, with the exception of some, who refused to leave their husbands. In some cases they were torn from their husbands and pushed into the boats, but in many instances they were allowed to remain, since there was no one to insist that they should go."

From Beesley's *The Loss of the* SS Titanic

Like the staterooms and lounges above the decks, the pantries and storerooms below were also lavishly stocked. Among the *Titanic*'s provisions on her maiden voyage were 75,000 pounds of fresh meat, 11,000 pounds of fresh fish, 1 ton of sausages, 40,000 fresh eggs, 40 tons of potatoes, 15,000 bottles of beer, 1,175 pounds of ice cream, 36,000 each of apples and oranges, 8,000 cigars, 57,600 items of crockery, 29,000 pieces of glassware, 44,000 pieces of cutlery (including 1,000 oyster forks), and 45,000 table napkins.

The Unsinkable and the Unthinkable

It was generally believed that the *Titanic* was unsinkable under any circumstances, a popular misconception that the White Star Line had

The *Titanic* was divided into sixteen watertight compartments by fifteen bulkheads with doors *(above)*. The night the ship sank, these doors closed in an attempt to control flooding. Too much water poured into the *Titanic* through the pierced hull, however, to save the ship from sinking.

no interest in correcting. Constructed with sixteen automatic watertight compartments, she could sustain flooding to any two compartments and still, the builders claimed, stay afloat. Even if three of the first five compartments were flooded, the *Titanic* would not go down. No one could imagine any disaster at sea this state-of-the-art luxury liner might encounter that could test her supposed unsinkability.

Unfortunately, at approximately 11:40 PM on the clear, cold night of April 14, 1912—the fifth day of her maiden voyage—the unimaginable happened to the *Titanic*.

2

The Maiden Voyage of the Titanic

At approximately noon on April 10, 1912, the *Titanic* set sail from Southampton, England, on her maiden voyage. She made stops at Cherbourg, France, and Queenstown, Ireland, to pick up additional passengers before embarking for her final destination, New York City, with 2,223 passengers and crew members aboard.

Sunday, April 14

11:30 PM

The *Californian* sends a message to the *Titanic* stating that it is surrounded by ice. The busy *Titanic* wireless operator cuts the message short.

The Millionaire's Captain and His Unsinkable Ship

It was only fitting that the *Titanic* sailed under the command of Captain Edward J. Smith, the senior captain of the White Star Line. He was known as the Millionaire's Captain, a favorite of the high-society passengers who enjoyed his good cheer. After a forty-year career at sea, this was to be Captain Smith's final voyage before retirement. No one questioned that this highly regarded and skilled sailor deserved to lead the greatest ship ever built through her maiden voyage. Whether or not he had mastered the skills necessary to navigate this new kind of superliner does remain an open question, however.

The *Titanic*'s voyage was to be Captain Edward J. Smith's final trip before his retirement.

High Society

In an age when society's "high class" bankers and industrialists were glamorous celebrities (similar to today's rock stars and movie stars), some of the richest people in the world—including the world's richest man, John Jacob Astor—were on the *Titanic*'s passenger list. In addition to Mr. and Mrs. Astor, the *Titanic*'s passenger list included industrialists such as Charles H. Hays, president of the Grand Trunk Railroad; steel magnate Arthur Ryerson; and Washington A. Roebling II, whose grandfather and uncle built the Brooklyn Bridge. Prominent members of the arts community, such as publisher Henry Sleeper Harper; Broadway producer Henry B. Harris and his wife; painter Frank Millet; writer Jacques Futrelle, also sailed on the *Titanic*. The passenger list also featured some of the most wealthy socialites of the day, including members of the Rothschild banking family; millionaire playboy Benjamin Guggenheim; and the wealthy co-owner of the Macy's department store, Isidor Straus, and his wife.

Edward J. Smith: Captain of the *Titanic*

"Men, you have done your full duty. You can do no more. Abandon your cabin. You look out for yourselves. I release you. That's the way of it at this kind of time. Every man for himself."

From Titanic: *An Illustrated History*

Sunday, April 14

11:40 PM

An iceberg is spotted, and the *Titanic* attempts to avoid it. It strikes the iceberg and the ship's hull is damaged.

Smooth Sailing

For all of the festivity and publicity, the *Titanic* was to make a fairly routine Atlantic crossing, one made year in and year out by hundreds of ships in all sorts of weather. Captain Smith, the experienced, veteran commander, was himself no stranger to the route that took them through well-charted and regularly traveled waters. Their course was west across the Atlantic Ocean from England to the Canadian province of Newfoundland on the east coast of North America, then south to New York.

In fact, the entire trip across the sea right up until the fateful hour on the night of April 14 was strictly routine. The weather was clear for virtually the entire voyage, the sea calm, and the winds light. The sun shined all day, and bright starlight made every night even more glittering than the sparkle provided by the ship's polished surfaces, electric lights, and festive socialites.

Ice Warnings

The first ice warnings were received by the *Titanic*'s wireless operator on Sunday, April 14. Ships in the area, including the *Baltic* of the White Star Line and the *Californian* of the Leyland Line, radioed in at least seven separate warnings, some concerning ice as close as five miles away from the *Titanic*'s planned course.

This is the area where the *Titanic* hit the iceberg that caused it to sink.

The *Titanic*'s radio operators logged the warnings and reported them to Captain Smith, but neither he nor the other officers seemed concerned. The ship was kept at her cruising speed of twenty-one knots and, other than ordering the crew members to keep a sharp lookout for ice, the watch was not increased. The temperature at sea was 31° Fahrenheit at 10:00 PM.

Captain Smith's calm was mirrored on both the water and in the ship's lounges. As the *Titanic* steamed across a placid North Atlantic at twenty-one or twenty-two knots, the passengers were relaxed, enjoying their adventure and all the amenities the ship had to offer. It had been a perfect voyage, justifying White Star's pride in the new queen of their line.

The "unsinkable" *Titanic*, however, was steaming ever closer to her deadly fate.

3

"A Night to Remember"

The *Titanic*'s maiden voyage was off to a spectacular start. The weather was glorious, the water untroubled. It seemed as if the *Titanic* would reach New York in record time. In the late afternoon of April 14, many passengers ventured out on the decks to gaze at a stunning sunset. Some remarked upon the growing coldness in the air. A few passengers with sailing experience claimed to smell ice. The thrill of sailing on such a grand ship in such beautiful weather, however, far outweighed any concern over the cold. They had no way of knowing that this carefree illusion of calm was about to be shattered.

"Iceberg Right Ahead!"

At 11:40 PM, some 400 miles off the coast of Newfoundland, lookout Frederick Fleet spotted an iceberg looming dead ahead in the frozen darkness. As later reported in the Senate inquiry into the sinking, he quickly phoned the bridge with the now famous words "Iceberg right ahead!" The officer on watch ordered the helmsman to turn the ship "hard a'starboard" and signaled the engine room to reverse the engines. This was meant to slow the *Titanic* and divert her bow from a head-on collision with the huge iceberg. Yet reversing the engines, while slowing the ship's forward motion, also slowed her ability to maneuver away from the iceberg, making a collision even more likely.

It took the mammoth *Titanic* almost forty seconds to respond to these ordered corrections. Suddenly, the ship's enormous size and speed were a liability rather than an asset; the huge, heavy ship was very hard to maneuver side to side quickly, especially when her engines were at full throttle. Just before the moment of impact with the iceberg, the *Titanic* began to swing to port. The ship's bow swept clear of the giant mountain of ice, but her starboard side scraped against it, tearing open what was long assumed to be a 300-foot gash across her first six watertight compartments.

Floodwaters and Distress Calls

Belowdecks, the *Titanic* had begun to take on water. Within minutes, fourteen feet of water filled the six ruptured watertight

Small tears in six of the *Titanic's* watertight compartments allow water to pour in at a rate of seven tons per second.

compartments. The watertight doors between these compartments had closed in an attempt to contain the leaking. With water rushing into each of them from the massive damage about twenty feet below the waterline on the starboard side of the bow, however, the doors proved useless. Too many compartments had been ruptured; the ship would surely sink after tipping forward on its flooded bow.

Even as the ship filled with hundreds of gallons of water, no alarm was sounded or warnings made to the ship's crew and passengers. Captain Smith assessed the damage with Thomas Andrews, the managing director of Harland and Wolff and the head of its design department, who estimated that the ship would be lying on the ocean floor in a little more than one hour. Upon receiving this grim news from the *Titanic's* builder, Smith ordered the radio operator to send the first distress call. It went out a few minutes after midnight on April 15 and was picked up by several nearby ships.

One of those hearing the call was the *Carpathia*, some fifty-eight miles southeast of the *Titanic*, which immediately turned around and sailed at top speed toward her. The *Carpathia's* captain ordered his crew to prepare the small steamship for rescue operations.

Another ship, the *Californian*, was even closer to the *Titanic* and, according to witnesses, had her in sight during the entire time she was going down. The *Titanic* fired eight emergency signal rockets that were observed from, but ignored by, the *Californian*, whose wireless set had been turned off the night before. Crew members of the

Californian later claimed they mistook the *Titanic* for a small steamer, and its flares for either a masthead light or flashes from a Morse-code lamp.

A Chaotic Evacuation

At 12:05 AM, Captain Smith ordered that the lifeboats be cleared, swung over the side of the ship, and readied for loading and lowering. Women and children were given first priority to enter the lifeboats. There was a lot of confusion about who was to go where, however, as the crew

This is a re-enactment of the scene in the wireless room of the SS *Carpathia*, where the *Titanic*'s distress signals were first received.

began to rouse sleeping passengers from their quarters. The crew had performed only one brief lifeboat drill (consisting of lowering two of the boats into the water) before the *Titanic* had sailed. No list had been posted that assigned specific crew members to specific lifeboat stations until several days into the voyage. Boats were not loaded in an orderly manner—as increasingly anxious passengers dashed from one deck to another and from boat to boat—and many were lowered into the ocean with far fewer occupants than they could safely carry. Although the lifeboats had the capacity to hold sixty-five people each, one was lowered with as few as twenty-one aboard, while others were sent down similarly underloaded. In the end, the lifeboats abandoned the *Titanic* with roughly 500 fewer passengers than they could hold.

Since there were not enough lifeboats to begin with, it was important that they be loaded to full capacity. The *Titanic* carried only sixteen lifeboats and four collapsible boats, enough to hold up to 1,178 people, and life vests for all on board. The ship had sailed with 2,223 people. Even though the *Titanic* was equipped to hold forty-eight boats, the sixteen lifeboats and four collapsible boats exceeded the minimum safety requirements of the British Board of Trade, which regulated that nation's shipping. Though grossly negligent, the *Titanic* was not in violation of any laws.

The number of lifeboats on the *Titanic* was woefully inadequate to save all of the ship's passengers. Some 80 percent of the men and 30 percent of the women on board perished.

And yet, for all the confusion and inefficiency, there was almost no panic reported among the first-class passengers. In the steerage section of the ship, however, there was great confusion and concern. Many of the passengers did not speak English and could not understand the instructions they were given by hurried stewards. Some accounts report that third-class passengers were physically barred from the first-class decks and the lifeboats until very late in the crisis. The White Star Line later denied that any attempts were made to keep third-class passengers from entering the lifeboats, but the fact remains that less than one-quarter of steerage passengers survived.

"So Will We Die"

Many tales of bravery and self-sacrifice were reported, including wives and children forced to leave husbands and fathers behind, wives who refused to be separated from their husbands, and people giving up seats on lifeboats to strangers. In Titanic: *An Illustrated History*, Don Lynch gives such an account. Ida Straus, wife of Isidor Straus, refused to be separated from him. When urged to enter a lifeboat, she said, "I will not be separated from my husband. As we have lived, so will we die together." It was then suggested that, given Straus's advanced age, no one would object if he accompanied his wife on a lifeboat. His reply: "I will not go before the other men." The couple was last seen sitting calmly together on a pair of deck chairs.

Several men from first class, unable to join their wives and children, dressed themselves in tuxedos and waited calmly for the end, seated on deck chairs or having one last cocktail in the lounge. Norris Williams, a tennis star, passed the time in the *Titanic*'s gymnasium with his father, where they rode stationary bikes to keep warm as the ship sank. He would later watch his father get crushed by the collapsing forward funnel of the ship. Norris was rescued by the *Carpathia* where a doctor recommended that his badly frozen legs be amputated. Norris refused and eventually regained his health and strength.

Monday, April 15

12:00 AM

Captain Smith radios a distress signal. At 12:05 he orders the uncovering of the lifeboats. Evacuation begins about twenty minutes later.

It was widely reported that the *Titanic*'s musicians began playing lively music in the first-class lounge in an effort to boost the spirits of the frightened passengers. As the situation worsened and the chaotic evacuation proceeded, the band came on deck to play soothing waltzes and religious hymns, continuing as the ship went down. This gave rise to the expression, "And the band played on . . ." None of the musicians survived, and none seemed to have tried to get on a lifeboat.

Survivors of the *Titanic* crowd a lifeboat in this photo taken from the deck of the *Carpathia*. Overall, the lifeboats abandoned the *Titanic* with roughly 500 fewer passengers than they could have held.

By 2:05 AM, the last lifeboat had pulled away from the *Titanic*. During the first hour, an estimated 25,000 tons of water had poured into the ship's bow, raising her stern higher and higher into the air. At 2:17 AM, the *Titanic* sent out her last call for help. According to Senate testimony, Captain Smith announced that it was now "every man for himself." The forward funnel collapsed, crushing several people. The ship's lights, having stayed on throughout the ordeal, finally went out.

The Death of the *Titanic*

With the lifeboats all lowered and away, the 1,500 people remaining on board (roughly 67 percent of the ship's passengers and crew members) could do nothing but gather together at the rapidly rising stern as the ship's bow disappeared beneath the waves. There was little anyone could do except jump clear before the great ship went under.

Survivors reported that the ship's stern rose straight up as the *Titanic* finally sank beneath the frigid North Atlantic waters, apparently intact, at approximately 2:20 AM. Though some experts believe that it could not have risen nearly so high, others claimed it broke in two before sinking. There is still debate about whether the *Titanic* broke in two before sinking, while sinking, or after hitting the ocean floor. One of the most popular theories is that the ship's stern rose higher and higher out of the water as its bow sank. At one point, the

Col. Archibald Gracie: Passenger

"There was nothing in sight save the ocean, dotted with ice and strewn with large masses of wreckage. Dying men and women all about me were groaning and crying piteously . . . Soon the raft became so full that it seemed as if she would sink if more came on board her . . . Many of those whom we refused answered as they went to their death, 'Good luck. God bless you!' "

From Gracie's *A Survivor's Story and the Sinking of the* SS Titanic

This undated drawing, entitled "The Doomed *Titanic*," depicts the final moments of the huge ship's plunge into the frigid waters of the North Atlantic as boatloads of survivors flee.

ship achieved a vertical position, with the stern sticking straight up out of the water. At this point, the ship snapped between the third and fourth funnels, and the bow sunk out of sight, though it may not have fully separated from the stern. The stern fell back onto the water in an almost normal, upright position. As it began filling with water, however, it again began rising out of the water and soon followed the bow on its two and one-half mile journey to the bottom of the sea.

And then, except for the increasingly faint screams and cries for help from the water and the slap of the frigid waves against the hulls of the wooden lifeboats, all was quiet.

4

What Went Wrong?

The *Carpathia* arrived on the scene a little after 4:00 AM and began the rescue efforts. For the next four hours, the survivors, who had spent the frigid night in lifeboats, were taken aboard the rescue ship, where every effort was made to provide them comfort and medical aide. Anyone who had not made it into a lifeboat had long since frozen to death in the icy waters of the North Atlantic.

Monday, April 15

12:45 AM

The first lifeboat and distress rocket are launched. Nineteen more lifeboats and seven more rockets will be launched over the next ninety minutes.

From Rescue to Recovery

The *Californian*, whose radio operator had come back on duty by the time the *Carpathia* began its rescue effort, arrived on the scene

Rescuers from the *Carpathia* help the *Titanic*'s radio operator, Harold Bride. Bride's SOS calls alerted the *Carpathia* to the sinking ship.

around 8:00 AM, after all survivors had been taken aboard the *Carpathia*. Although in sight of the *Titanic* during the sinking and its aftermath, the *Californian* did not arrive on the scene to offer help until eight and one-half hours after the ship struck the iceberg and began sending distress signals, and six and one-half hours after it sunk altogether. While the *Carpathia* sailed for New York with the survivors, the *Californian* stayed in the area to conduct a belated but thorough search for additional survivors and bodies.

But there was no one left to save. The *Carpathia* carried all 706 survivors; the remaining 1,517 passengers and crew perished. Only one out of three people who boarded the *Titanic* lived to see New York Harbor. Floating bodies continued to be discovered by passing ships as late as June, two months after the disaster. Many of the retrieved bodies were dressed warmly, and their pockets were often stuffed with meat, biscuits, tobacco, large sums of cash, and even diamonds.

Separating Truth from Rumor: The Investigation

The *Carpathia* arrived in New York on the evening of April 18. By this time, several days after the supposedly unsinkable *Titanic* had gone down, the ship's fate had made headlines around the world. Details were still sketchy and could not be verified until survivors were interviewed. Misinformation and rumors ran wild—even among survivors and eyewitnesses—including unsubstantiated claims that the captain and some officers had committed suicide as the ship went down and that some passengers were shot by crewmen when they rushed toward the lifeboats. Some early newspaper accounts of the accident reported that all of the passengers and crew were saved before the ship went down. Others claimed the *Titanic* left behind no survivors. Most, however, told a story closer to the truth: Some, but not nearly all, were saved and would be returning home.

Monday, April 15

2:20 AM

The *Titanic* sinks after its lights blink out and its stern rises in the air and partially tears away from the bow.

The events leading up to the collision at sea and the aftermath were pieced together by the press and official British and American investigations that followed. The United States Senate Committee on Commerce conducted a hearing on the accident that lasted eighteen days. Eighty-six witnesses—including passengers and crew members, the ship's four surviving officers, and J. Bruce Ismay, managing director of the White Star Line, who had been a passenger on the *Titanic*'s ill-fated voyage—provided over 1,000 pages of testimony.

The *Titanic*'s third officer, H. J. Pitman, takes the stand at the Senate inquiry into the sinking of the ship. Pitman oversaw the loading and lowering of the first lifeboat to leave the *Titanic* and served as its commander throughout the long night in the icy water.

J. Bruce Ismay: Managing Director of the White Star Line

"Deeply regret advise you *Titanic* sank this morning after collision iceberg, resulting serious loss of life. Full particulars later. Bruce Ismay."

Cable sent to New York from J. Bruce Ismay, managing director of the White Star Line

From Titanic: *An Illustrated History*

Placing Blame

The Senate committee's conclusions were issued on May 28, 1912. It placed the blame on several factors, not the least of which was Captain Smith himself, who apparently went down with the ship. Though full of praise for the captain's long and distinguished career, the committee concluded that he had been guilty of overconfidence in his ship and a resulting reckless disregard for danger.

Captain Smith had, in other words, been aware of but ignored repeated radio warnings of icebergs in the vicinity of the *Titanic*. And even though aware, the captain took no steps to increase the watch for ice. Senate testimony revealed that, only hours before the accident, the steamship *Californian* had wired the *Titanic* via a relay station in Cape Race, Newfoundland, "We are stopped and surrounded by ice." The radio operator of the *Titanic* responded, "Shut up! Shut up! I am busy. I am working [sending passenger messages to] Cape Race." Nor did Captain Smith reduce speed in these treacherous waters; the *Titanic* was steaming ahead at twenty-one or twenty-two knots, her fastest speed of the voyage, at the time of the collision. It is generally thought that Captain Smith was operating under extreme pressure from Ismay to reach New York a day early and beat the crossing time of the *Titanic's* sister ship, the *Olympic*.

In addition to the poor decision making of Captain Smith, the bulk of the remaining blame for the sinking was placed on the catastrophic damage to the hull inflicted by the iceberg and the resulting flooding of the ship. The *Titanic's* fate was sealed as soon as she struck the iceberg; nothing any crew member could have done would have prevented the ship's sinking at that point.

J. Bruce Ismay *(right)* and one of his attorneys leave the Senate office building after testifying before the Senate subcommittee investigating the *Titanic* disaster.

Never Again

In addition to the causes of the accident, the Senate inquiry pinpointed several key reasons for the massive loss of life that resulted from it. Not the least of these was the *Titanic's* failure to carry enough lifeboats for the safety of her passengers. It was recommended that a statute be passed requiring all ships entering U.S. ports to provide enough lifeboats for every single passenger on board (a step the White Star Line had already taken on all its ships immediately following the accident).

The inquiry also noted that the *Titanic* had not held adequate lifeboat drills before sailing, and that neither crew nor passengers had been given lifeboat assignments. Under new regulations, crews were required to perform lifeboat drills at least twice a month. Passengers were also to be drilled and lifeboat assignments were to be posted before sailing.

At the time of the *Titanic* sinking, wireless radio (which could send and receive messages) was a relatively new addition to ships and was used largely as a convenience for passengers trying to send messages to shore. Radios were not required on ships, and those that did have them did not keep them switched on all the time. That is why the *Titanic*'s distress call was not heard by the nearby *Californian*. After the *Titanic*, ships were required to be equipped with a wireless that was monitored twenty-four hours a day by operators.

In addition to changes in ship operations, many design changes to ocean liners were also introduced to help prevent another accident of such magnitude. New ships would feature watertight skins and watertight compartments, bulkheads, and decks, designed in light of what had been learned from the failure of the *Titanic*'s design.

Almost as soon as it came to rest on the ocean floor off the coast of Newfoundland, the *Titanic* was to rise to the status of legend. The *Titanic* grew from a glittering symbol of the Gilded Age from which she

Conclusion

sailed into an icon of the deadly modernity she seemed to herald, as the years following her sinking would see the great stock market crash, a worldwide economic depression, two world wars, the Holocaust, and a growing nuclear menace.

The *Titanic* Returns

The true extent of the damage done to the *Titanic* remained a mystery that many believed would never be solved. The exact location of the ship was unknown, and she was, at any rate, resting more than two miles below the surface of the ocean. While many searched for the lost ship, few believed she would ever be found.

However, on July 5, 1985, a joint French-American scientific expedition led by Dr. Robert Ballard of the Woods Hole Oceanographic Institution in Massachusetts, set out to find what had been lost seventy-three years earlier. Utilizing sonar, imaging devices, unmanned submersible crafts, and underwater cameras,

A piece of the *Titanic's* hull is raised to the ocean's surface off the coast of St. John's, Newfoundland, on August 10, 1998.

Ballard and his team systematically searched the area where the *Titanic* was believed to have gone down. When she was eventually located, on September 1, 1985, the *Titanic* was two and one-half miles to the south and fifteen and one-half miles to the east of her last reported position, about 375 miles off the coast of Newfoundland.

New Answers to Old Questions

What Ballard and his associates found answered many of the mysteries surrounding the fate of the *Titanic*. Her last minutes had been violently destructive. Computer simulations based on what was already known and Ballard's new data showed that the ship was tearing apart just before it finally sank, her water-filled bow pulling away from the stern. The ship was also bending in the middle from the staggering weight of the water flooding into her. The *Titanic* broke in two after she sank below the ocean's surface, either on her way down or when she hit the ocean floor where she came to rest, some 12,500 feet below. The two halves of the ship landed less than 2,000 feet apart, with a field of debris—everything from broken pieces of the hull to cabin furniture to cutlery—stretched between them.

It had long been believed that the iceberg had ripped a 300-foot gash in the hull. Investigation of the wreckage showed, however, that rather than creating a single, huge gash, the collision caused a series of small tears in the hull as the *Titanic* bumped and scraped along the ice. Some of these rips were no more than an inch wide, but they occurred where the plates of the hull had been riveted together.

Many of the *Titanic's* victims are buried at three cemeteries in Halifax, Nova Scotia. The Baron De Hirsch Cemetery holds Jewish victims, the Mount Olivet Cemetery holds Catholic victims, and the Fairview Lawn Cemetery holds others.

Samples of steel from the hull brought up from the wreck of the *Titanic* underwent metallurgical analysis. The results, published in the *Journal of Metals*, showed the steel was contaminated with high levels of sulfur, oxygen, and phosphorus, making it vulnerable to fracturing under impact, especially in cold temperatures. The icy waters of the North Atlantic had made the ship's hull brittle. When the frozen steel slammed against the iceberg, rivets holding the steel plates to the ship popped, allowing the plates to pull apart. Even the rivets themselves are now believed to have been defective, at least by modern standards. Those few that have been recovered and examined (out of some three million used in her construction) show signs of having been contaminated with slag (the waste product that results from the melting of metals), which would have weakened them.

Lessons Learned

It would be years until the devices that now make travel by sea so much safer would be developed and put to use, thanks largely to the lessons taught by the *Titanic* disaster. Modern passenger liners—not to mention military and commercial ships—are equipped with radar, sonar, and satellite positioning technology. Captains can see at a glance what is around, beneath, and approaching them from a great distance. Their exact position, accurate to within inches in the middle of a vast ocean, is logged by satellites orbiting high above the earth. Radar will warn them of icebergs long before they will ever be able to see them with their own eyes. Real-time weather maps from satellites show captains exactly what conditions they are sailing into.

As for the *Titanic*, she will remain where she was found, 12,500 feet (or two and one-half miles) below the ocean's surface, a silent monument to human endeavor and a haunting memorial to human failure.

Glossary

beam   The width of a ship at its widest point.

bow   The front section of a ship or boat.

helmsman   A person who steers a ship.

hull   The frame or body of a ship, not including masts, sails, yards, and rigging.

keel   The principal structural part of a ship, running lengthwise along the center line from bow to stern to which the frame is attached.

knot   Nautical unit of speed equal to approximately 1.15 miles per hour; thus 10 knots equals 11.5 miles per hour.

metallurgical analysis   The knowledge and study of metals at the atomic level.

port   The left-hand side of a ship as one faces forward.

slag   The vitreous, or glasslike, mass left as a residue by the smelting of metallic ore.

sonar   A system using transmitted and reflected sound waves to detect and locate submerged objects.

starboard   The right-hand side of a ship as one faces forward.

stern   The rear part of a ship or boat.

watertight compartment   Sealed section of a ship's hull, designed to contain water in one area and prevent its spread throughout the ship.

wireless   A radio telegraph or telephone system.

FOR MORE INFORMATION

British *Titanic* Society
P.O. Box 401
Hope Carr Way
Leigh, Lancashire WN7 3WW
United Kingdom

RMS *Titanic*, Inc. (the only company with salvage
rights to the *Titanic*)
3340 Peachtree Road NE, Suite 1225
Atlanta, GA 30326
(404) 842-2600
(800) TITANIC (848-2642)
Web site: http://www.titanic-online.com

Titanic Historical Society and Museum
208 Main Street
Indian Orchard, MA 01151-0053
(413) 543-4770
Web site: http://www.titanic1.org

Ulster *Titanic* Society
P.O. Box 401
Carrickfergus BT38 8US
Northern Ireland
Web site: http://www.nireland.com/uts

Web Sites

Due to the changing nature of Internet links, the Rosen Publishing Group, Inc., has developed an online list of Web sites related to the subject of this book. This site is updated regularly. Please use this link to access the list:

http://www.rosenlinks.com/wds/trti/

For Further Reading

Ballard, Robert D. *Exploring the* Titanic. Glenview, IL: Scott Foresmen, 1993.

Brewster, Hugh, and Laurie Coulter. *882 1/2 Amazing Answers to Your Questions About the* Titanic. New York: Scholastic Trade, 1999.

Geller, Judith B., and John P. Eaton. Titanic: *Women and Children First.* New York: W.W. Norton and Co., 1998.

Landau, Elaine, and Jim Burke. *Heroine of the* Titanic: *The Real Unsinkable Molly Brown.* New York: Clarion Books, 2001.

Lord, Walter. *A Night to Remember.* New York: Bantam Books, 1997.

Lynch, Don. Titanic: *An Illustrated History.* New York: Hyperion, 1997.

Pellegrino, Charles R. *Her Name,* Titanic: *The Untold Story of the Sinking and Finding of the Unsinkable Ship.* New York: Avon, 1997.

White, Ellen Emerson, ed. *Voyage on the Great* Titanic: *The Diary of Margaret Ann Brady, R.M.S.* Titanic, *1912.* New York: Scholastic, 1998.

Bibliography

Ballard, Robert D., and Rick Archbold. *The Discovery of the* Titanic. New York: Warner Books, 1995.

Beesley, Lawrence. *The Loss of the SS* Titanic: *Its Story and Its Lessons.* New York: Houghton Mifflin Co., 2000.

Brown, David G. *The Last Log of the* Titanic. New York: McGraw-Hill Professional Publishing, 2000.

Eaton, John P., and Charles A. Haas. Titanic: *Destination Disaster: The Legends and the Reality.* New York: W.W. Norton and Co., 1996.

Geller, Judith B., and John P. Eaton. Titanic: *Women and Children First.* New York: W.W. Norton and Co., 1998.

Gracie, Archibald. Titanic: *A Survivor's Story and the Sinking of the SS* Titanic. Chicago: Academy Chicago Publications, 1998.

Kuntz, Tom, ed. *The* Titanic *Disaster Hearings: The Official Transcripts of the 1912 Senate Investigation.* New York: Pocket Books, 1998.

Lord, Walter. *A Night to Remember.* New York: Bantam Books, 1997.

Lynch, Don. Titanic: *An Illustrated History.* New York: Hyperion, 1997.

McCaughan, Michael. *The Birth of the* Titanic. Montreal: McGill-Queens University Press, 1999.

McCluskie, Tom. *Anatomy of the* Titanic. San Diego, CA: Thunder Bay Press, 1998.

Mowbray, Jay Henry, ed. *The Sinking of the* Titanic: *Eyewitness Accounts*. New York: Dover Publications, 1998.

Quinn, Paul J. *Dusk to Dawn: Survivor Accounts of the Last Night on the* Titanic. Hollis, NH: Fantail, 1999.

Wels, Susan. Titanic: *Legacy of the World's Greatest Ocean Liner*. New York: Time Life, 1997.

Index

About the Author

Paul Kupperberg is a freelance writer and editor for DC Comics. He has published more than 700 comic books, stories, books, and articles, as well as several years' worth of the newspaper comic strips *Superman* and *Tom and Jerry*. Paul lives in Connecticut with his wife, Robin, and son, Max.

Photo Credits

Cover, pp. 6, 12, 39 © Ralph White/Corbis; inset cover photo, pp. 1, 23, 24, 28, 32 © Bettmann/Corbis; pp. 4–5, 14 © The Mariners' Museum, Newport News, VA; p. 10 © Corbis; p. 16 © Timepix; pp. 19, 26, 30 © Getty Images; p. 34 © Underwood and Underwood/Corbis; p. 37 © AP/Wide World Photos/Discovery Channel/RMS *Titanic* Inc.

Series Design and Layout

Les Kanturek

A POSITIVE SUPERHERO

Growing Up with HIV

by

Desiree Thompson

Library of Congress Cataloging-in-Publication Data
Thompson, Desiree.
A Positive Superhero: Growing Up with HIV - First edition.

Library of Congress Control Number: 2015915493
CreateSpace Independent Publishing Platform, North Charleston, SC

ISBN-10: 1505498325
ISBN-13: 978-1505498325

Summary: James is growing up with HIV and explains to young readers his medical condition in a way they are able to understand. He is strong, brave, responsible, and heroic! This story encourages others to not be afraid of those who are medically different.

The illustrations in this book were done in Inkscape and were based on images created by Desiree Thompson.

The text type was set in Gadugi and Showcard Gothic (title).

Printed in the United States of America by CreateSpace, An Amazon.com Company

For Tariku,
My little superhero.

And for children everywhere who live with HIV.

Many thanks to my wonderful husband who graciously gave me time to work on this project.

Special thanks to my group of friends who acted as my editors, encouragers, and support throughout this process.

Hi. My name is James.

I like running and racing. Most of the time my friends can't catch me because I am SUPER-FAST!

When I grow up I am going to be a superhero.

When I am a superhero, I will use my speed
to save the world by catching bad guys.

There is one thing that makes me different than some of my friends. I have a virus in my body called HIV.

0

HIV is a virus that acts
like a villain living
inside of me.

11

When I was little, my virus grew strong and multiplied. It started to take over. This made me really sick and slow. I didn't like how the virus made me feel.

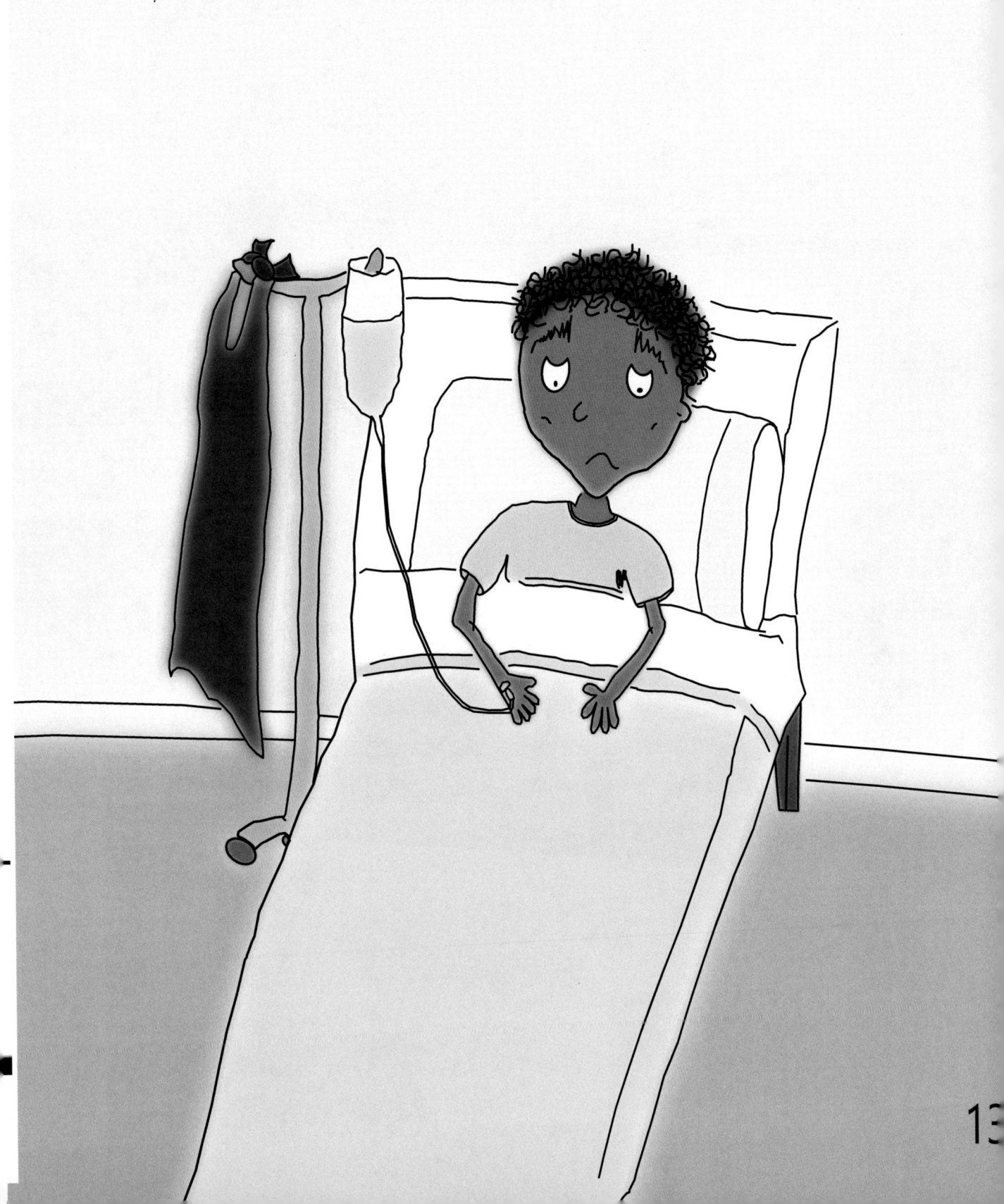

To fight off the HIV in my body I take medicine called antiretroviral drugs (or ARV's). I take my pills every morning at the same time, when I eat breakfast. That way I am energized for the day.

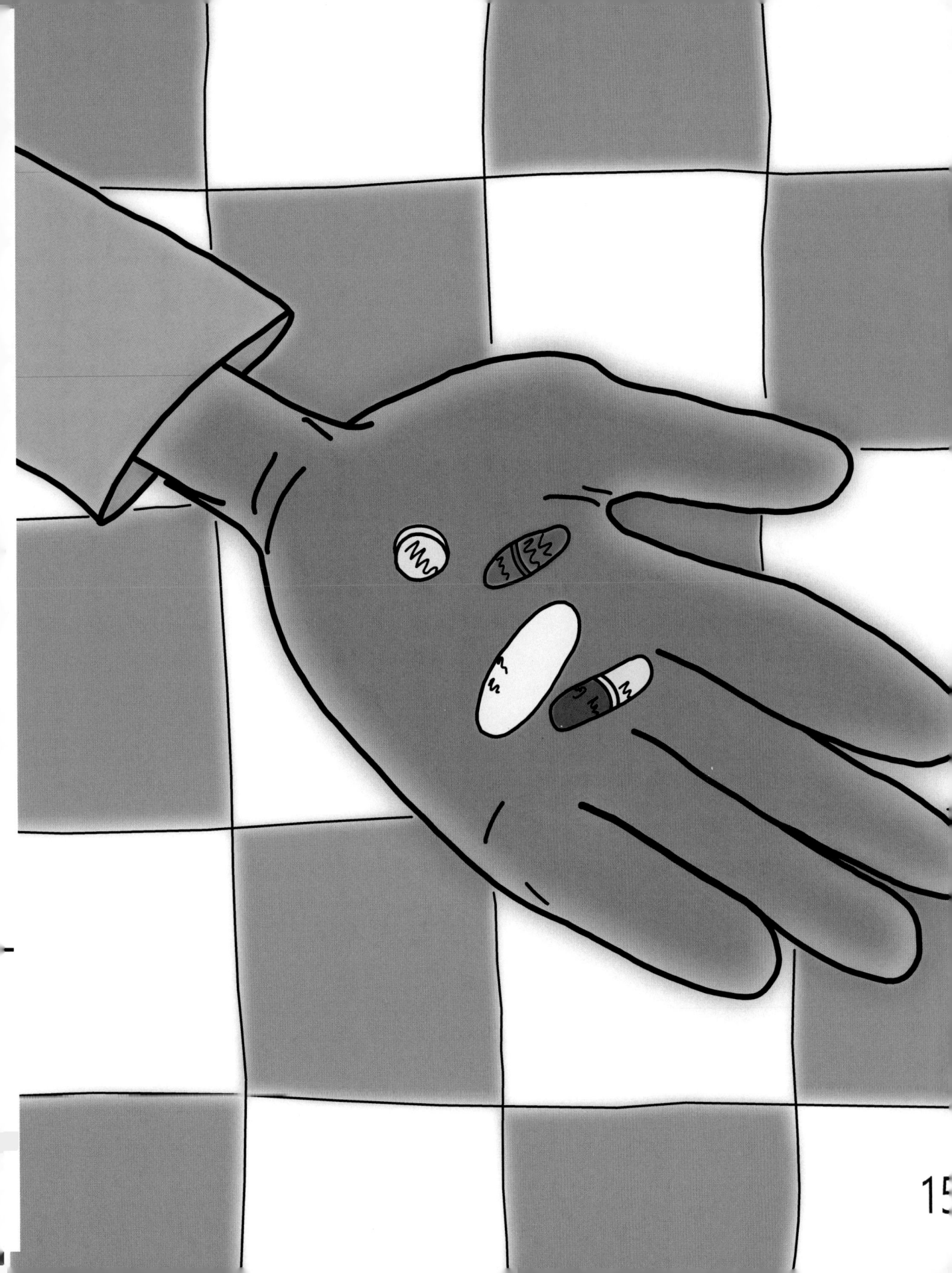

My medicine has special powers
that keep my HIV under control so
that I am not sick anymore.

Now my virus is contained, and
it can't take over my body.

This lets me zoom around and
look out for *bad guys.

*The "bad guy" in this picture is just
my friend pretending to be a villian.

19

Every few months I have to get my blood drawn. This is when a nurse takes a sample of my blood to see how much of the virus is inside of my body. The needle poke hurts a little. I have to sit still and be really brave just like a real superhero. My nurse tells me I am heroic.

After each blood draw, my mom hugs me and tells me she is proud of me.

Along with taking my medicine and having blood draws, I see a special doctor a few times a year. My doctor tells me how much HIV is living in my body and how well my medicine is working. If there are any problems, he switches my medicine. Managing HIV is not hard, I usually forget I have the virus.

Some people are afraid of HIV.
They think they might catch my
virus and get sick.

HIV is not scary, no one can get
HIV from being my friend.

I was born with HIV. No one would ever know by looking at me because I am healthy and active. I will always have HIV because there is no medicine that wipes out the virus completely. Maybe some day there will be!

My Mom and Dad say I don't have to wait until I am big to be a superhero.

I already am a superhero by fighting my virus everyday!

29

About the Author & Illustrator

Desiree Thompson's mission is to educate everyone she meets with the truths of HIV and AIDS. She was exposed to the unfair stigma of living with HIV and AIDS during several trips to Ethiopia. She witnessed how HIV has many misconceptions and those with the disease are often treated unfairly. The need for accurate information to be distributed weighed heavily on her heart. She especially wanted to focus on helping kids understand that living with HIV should not include living with the stigma that surrounds this chronic disease.

A resident in a small town in Wisconsin, Mrs. Thompson is a full time wife, mother, teacher (homeschooling her children), and truth teller.

This is her first published book.

Write to James!

James loves to get positive mail. He regularly connects with other children that are living superheroes just like him. If you want to send him an encouraging note, stop by the author's website.

www.desiree-thompson.com

Helpful Resources

The information on this page is helpful in understanding HIV at a mature level. The resources provided are wonderful in helping those with HIV/AIDS. Please note that this book is not endorsed by or affiliated with any of the organizations listed.

HIV: Human Immunodeficiency Virus. HIV is the infection that causes AIDS. HIV weakens your immune system by attacking cells that fight infection.

AIDS: Acquired Immuno Deficiency Syndrome. You are medically diagnosed with AIDS when your immune system is weakened from the HIV infection to a point where your body is at risk for many potentially deadly diseases.

How is HIV spread?
*Unprotected sexual intercourse with someone who has HIV or AIDS.
*Mother to child transmission during pregnancy, childbirth, or breastfeeding if the mother has HIV or AIDS and is not on medication.
*Needles or syringes with someone who has HIV or AIDS.

You cannot get HIV from....
*shaking hands
*hugging
*kissing
*sharing a cup, plate, or fork with someone who has HIV
*using the same bathroom
*getting a cold from an HIV infected person
*insect bites
*saliva
*tears
*sweat
*playing tag
*being a friend

United States: AIDS.gov
HIV/AIDS information from the federal government about prevention, testing, treatment, research, and new media in response to HIV/AIDS. www.aids.gov

AVERT
AVERT is an international HIV and AIDS charity, based in the UK, working to avert HIV and AIDS worldwide, through education, treatment, and care. www.avert.org

Bethany Christian Services HIV Toolkit
This HIV toolkit is specifically designed to prepare and inform potential adoptive families in the challenges and blessings when considering adopting a child living with HIV. Each tool presents a hopeful yet realistic look at some of the challenges families may face.
www.bethany.org/resources/adoption-resources/hiv-resources

Children's Hospital of Wisconsin, Infectious Disease
The Pediatric Infectious Disease Program at Children's is committed to comprehensive and specialized medical care for children and youth with chronic and acute infectious disease. They have a comprehensive program for children, youth, women, and pregnant women living with HIV infection.
www.chw.org/medical-care/infectious-diseases/

Made in the USA
Coppell, TX
06 August 2022